Searching for Grace

A PANDEMIC MEDITATION ON THE HEBREW ALPHABET

Eugenia Koukounas

Full Court Press
Englewood Cliffs, New Jersey

First Edition

Copyright © 2020 by Eugenia Koukounas

All rights reserved. No part of this book may be reproduced or transmitted in any form or by any means electronic or mechanical, including by photocopying, by recording, or by any information storage and retrieval system, without the express permission of the author, except where permitted by law.

Published in the United States of America
by Full Court Press, 601 Palisade Avenue,
Englewood Cliffs, NJ 07632
fullcourtpress.com

ISBN 978-1-946989-76-5
Library of Congress Control Number: 2020917452

All art by the author

Editing and book design by Barry Sheinkopf

THIS BOOK IS AN ACTIVE PRAYER
FOR THOSE WHO NEED IT MOST

Venturing out to the mailbox,
How delightful to see a bumble bee—
A sudden, surprising splash of yellow
In the bristles of a bottle brush plant.

We've grown used to not noticing
Shadows shifting imperceptibly,
the deep coppery glow that gilds
summer evenings as the stars appear.

But after many weeks of sheltering,
we're witnessing a subtle change
in our collective breathing as we begin
at last to trust what's always there.

—Robert Lavett Smith,
"What's Always There"

PREFACE

When the coronavirus quarantine began and the news covering the pandemic grew more and more alarming, my initial reaction was to seek protection. I reached for my Bible and started reading the Book of Psalms, which has been my comfort for years. After a good half hour, though, I closed the book feeling somewhat dissatisfied. I realized that coming from a place of fear was not how I wanted to approach the crisis. I was going to have to come up with some other way to mobilize myself into action.

Though raised as a Greek Orthodox Christian, I attended a Catholic high school. I was taking a religion class—curious, interested—when the teacher, one of the older nuns teaching at the school, saw I made the sign of the cross "wrong." (In the Orthodox religion, one crosses from the right shoulder to the left.) She asked, "You're not a Christian, are you?"

Not Catholic, I was not obliged to take religion class and eventually chose not to. Yet my biology teacher, Sister Janine, insisted I meet her during my free period to study with her, one-on-one, the philosophy of Pierre Teilhard de Chardin. I found what she taught really engaging and was glad, in the long run, that she had badgered me into taking up her offer. During one of those sessions, she explained, "Praying isn't just putting your hands together and asking for something. You can pray by dedicating an hour, a day, or a week, to something. Or dedicate an action as prayer."

Her words came back to me as I considered how next to express my faith in the simple tenet "all will be well, world without end." Having studied Kabbalah more than a decade and a half, I remembered that, years ago, I had bought a roll of white paper fifteen inches by thirty feet with the intention of exploring the Hebrew alphabet.

I took the roll out of the back of my closet and initiated my effort by dedicating the work I was about to start as a prayer for anyone who needed it: I had decided to use my love of the sacred to think about others instead of myself.

But I had to face the empty expanse of this roll of paper, which intimidated me and was why it had been left untouched for years. What if I did it wrong, or, worse, not perfectly? Constantly frightening myself into inaction by the horror of being incapable of perfection made starting any artistic endeavor almost impossible.

I needed to give myself permission to make mistakes. I decided to use this as an opportunity to learn from any mistakes I made and, as I pushed onward through the alphabet, ultimately see that unintended beauty.

I included in the scroll excepts from the prologue of the Zohar—one of the more important books of Kabbalah—and in this volume I retell the story of God contemplating which letter of the Hebrew alphabet he intended to choose to create the world.

I copied Psalm 119 from the Old Testament (the King James Version), in which eight verses are dedicated to each letter of the Hebrew alphabet. And while it is a very long psalm in praise of God, I have always felt while reading it that the Hebrew letters that head their assigned verses gently influence me for the better—a purification process of sorts.

Finally, in addition to making copies of each letter, I tried my hand at fashioning some artistic expression of each letter, which has a certain energy and, therefore, its challenge to face.

As I worked through the alphabet, the letters became harder to master. While the first couple were easy to replicate and fashion art for, the farther along I got, the more effort they took. For instance, Pey, which is about humility and spiritual possibility, or Shin, highest intuition (both complex letter designs), did not come easy. I practiced getting the proportions of all the letters correct by writing them over and over again as a form of meditation until I felt I could replicate them correctly with a certain degree of uniformity.

I can't say whether this effort amounted to me learning to perfect the execution of letters or the letters were perfecting bits and pieces of me. I'd say probably both.

This book is a much-abbreviated version of the thirty-foot scroll I completed, which contains a great deal of extra information and was too unwieldy to convert.

Both have been a privilege to work on. My wish is that *Searching for Grace* gives the reader the same sense of joy that it gives me, and with joy, also a sense of peace and well-being. May the energy of these letters bring you to a better place. *Amen. Selah.*

—E.K.
West New York,
September 2020

"The human impulse to create and find meaning is a gift of grace."

—*Karen Swallow Prior*

After God has already said no to every letter except Beth, Aleph stands by silently. God asks why she has not come before Him as the other letters have. Aleph answers, "You've chosen Beth to begin the world, so there's no need for me to ask you, Lord." God replies that, while Beth will begin the creation of the world, *Bereshith bara*, Aleph will be first among the letters, and everything else shall begin with Aleph.

Psalm 119, verses 1–8
ALEPH

1 Blessed are the undefiled in the way, who walk in the law of the Lord.

2 Blessed are they that keep his testimonies, and that seek him with the whole heart.

3 They also do no iniquity: they walk in his ways.

4 Thou hast commanded us to keep thy precepts diligently.

5 O that my ways were directed to keep thy statutes!

6 Then shall I not be ashamed, when I have respect unto all thy commandments.

7 I will praise thee with uprightness of heart, when I shall have learned thy righteous judgments.

8 I will keep thy statutes: O forsake me not utterly.

Aleph means "ox" in Hebrew, which is a symbol of power, a source of wealth as well as creative energy. The letter expresses the quality of enlightened intellect and intuition. Its color is bright blue, and it rules the lungs. After birth, the first thing a newborn does is take a breath. To start any kind of meditation, one therefore takes a breath.

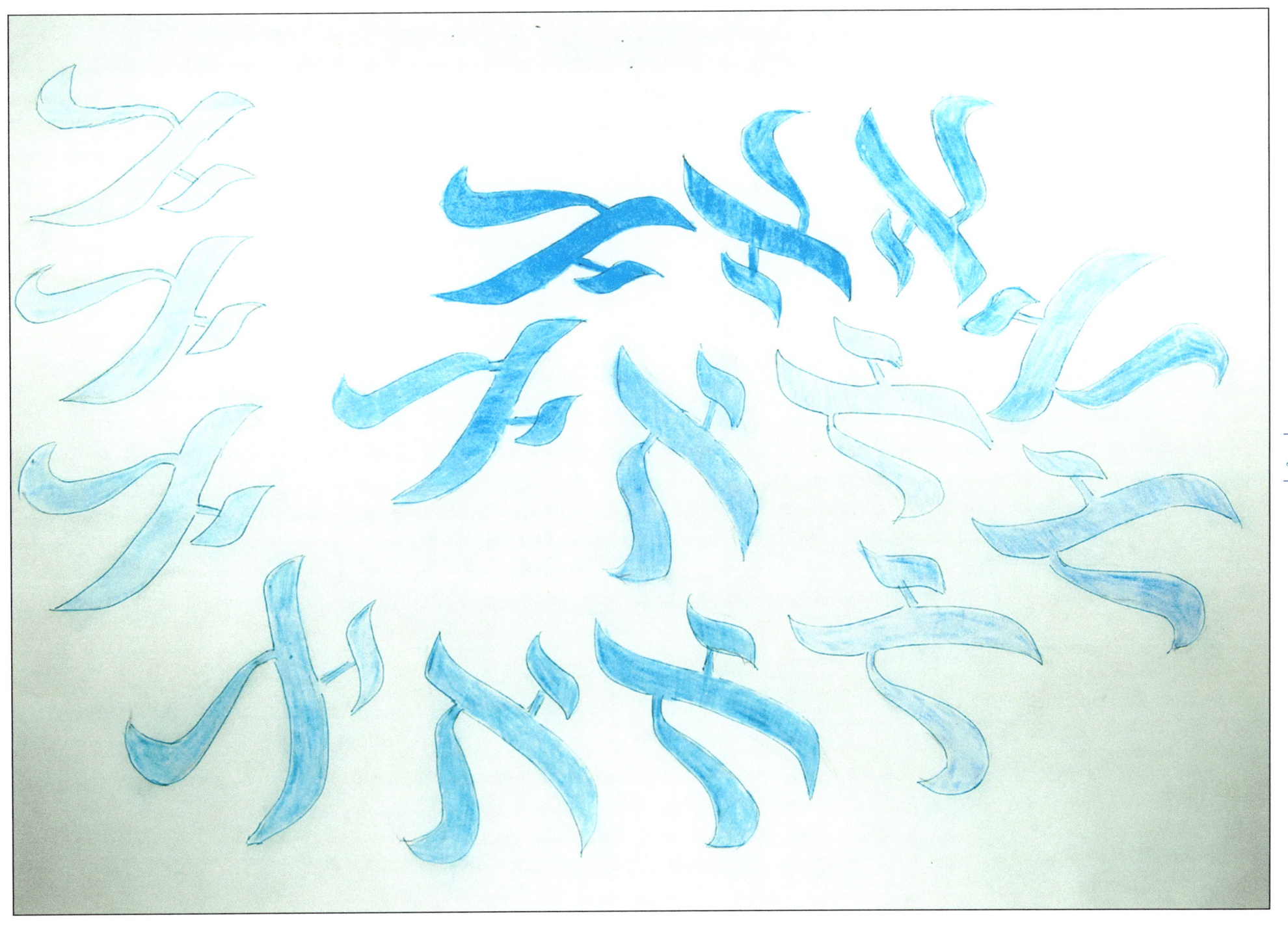

BETH COMES BEFORE GOD and asks to be chosen to create the world. God says yes because Beth is the initial letter of the word "blessings", *berakhoth*. And so Genesis begins with *Bereshit bara*, in the beginning....

Psalm 119, verses 9–16

BETH

9 Wherewithal shall a young man cleanse his way? by taking heed thereto according to thy word.

10 With my whole heart have I sought thee: O let me not wander from thy commandments.

11 Thy word have I hid in mine heart, that I might not sin against thee.

12 Blessed art thou, O Lord: teach me thy statutes.

13 With my lips have I declared all the judgments of thy mouth.

14 I have rejoiced in the way of thy testimonies, as much as in all riches.

15 I will meditate in thy precepts, and have respect unto thy ways.

16 I will delight myself in thy statutes: I will not forget thy word.

Beth means "house" is Hebrew, a place where we feel safe, where we begin our day, and certainly during the pandemic it is the center of our life. Beth possesses the quality to harmonize our entire emotional system. In order to begin to heal, to be centered in our lives, we need to get our emotions under control. Beth rules the right eye and is the color of bright violet.

Gimel, along with Daleth, approaches God to be considered as the letter with which to create the world. God says no because neither letter can stand on its own, so they cannot be separated from one another. For this reason, the two letters should be content with the task of supporting one another.

Psalm 119, verses 17–24
GIMEL

17 Deal bountifully with thy servant, that I may live, and keep thy word.

18 Open thou mine eyes, that I may behold wondrous things out of thy law.

19 I am a stranger in the earth: hide not thy commandments from me.

20 My soul breaketh for the longing that it hath unto thy judgments at all times.

21 Thou hast rebuked the proud that are cursed, which do err from thy commandments.

22 Remove from me reproach and contempt; for I have kept thy testimonies.

23 Princes also did sit and speak against me: but thy servant did meditate in thy statutes.

24 Thy testimonies also are my delight and my counsellors.

Gimel, in Hebrew, means "camel". Since Hebrew developed in a land where camels were associated with commerce and travel, Gimel expresses the concept of success and endurance, to finish the course of any task you choose and do so successfully. It rules the left eye. It is the color of grassy green.

DALETH AND GIMEL STAND before God and ask to be considered as the letter to initiate the creation of the world. God observes that Daleth begins the word *dalluth*, meaning "poverty" in Hebrew, which God points out will always exist, while Gimel begins the word *gemul,* which means "benefactor". Therefore, neither can be separated from the other because they will always maintain one another, and that alone should be enough for them both.

Psalm 119, verses 25–32
DALETH

25 My soul cleaveth unto the dust: quicken thou me according to thy word.

26 I have declared my ways, and thou heardest me: teach me thy statutes.

27 Make me to understand the way of thy precepts: so shall I talk of thy wondrous works.

28 My soul melteth for heaviness: strengthen thou me according unto thy word.

29 Remove from me the way of lying: and grant me thy law graciously.

30 I have chosen the way of truth: thy judgments have I laid before me.

31 I have stuck unto thy testimonies: O LORD, put me not to shame.

32 I will run the way of thy commandments, when thou shalt enlarge my heart.

Daleth means "door" in Hebrew. It therefore contains the quality that opens the door to facilitate any endeavor. It fuels spiritual development by opening up concepts about how the laws of the universe work. It rules the right ear, and is the color dark blue.

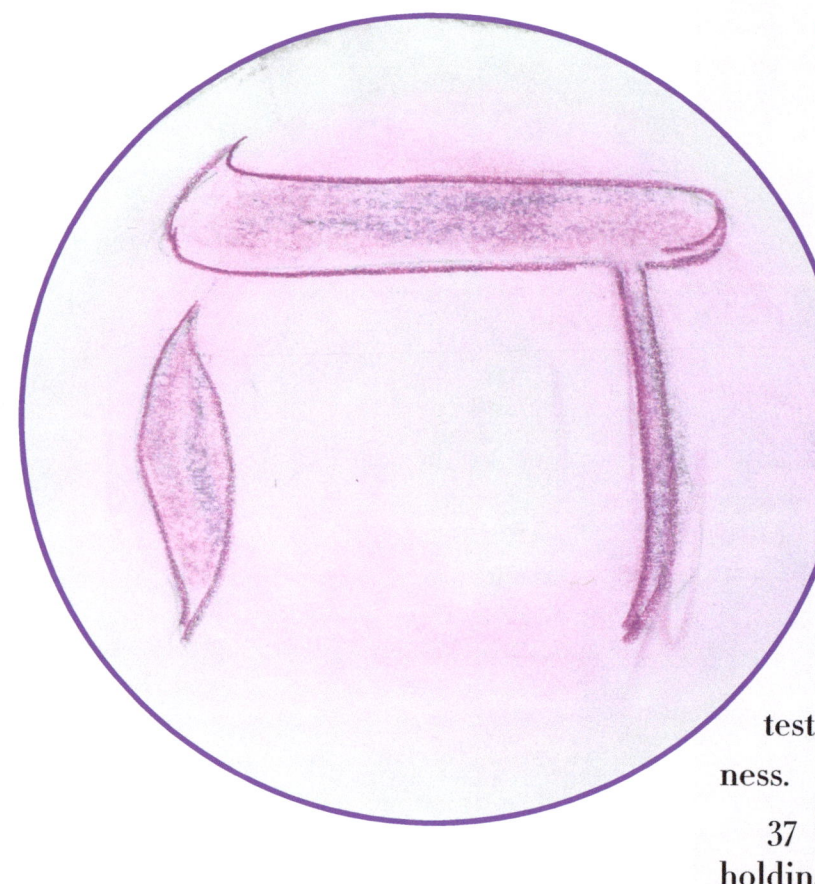

GOD SAYS NO TO BOTH HEY and Vav because they are letters that make up His name, Yehovah (YHVH) and therefore cannot be used to create the world.

Psalm 119, verses 33–40
HEY

33 Teach me, O LORD, the way of thy statutes; and I shall keep it unto the end.

34 Give me understanding, and I shall keep thy law; yea, I shall observe it with my whole heart.

35 Make me to go in the path of thy commandments; for therein do I delight.

36 Incline my heart unto thy testimonies, and not to covetousness.

37 Turn away mine eyes from beholding vanity; and quicken thou me in thy way.

38 Stablish thy word unto thy servant, who is devoted to thy fear.

39 Turn away my reproach which I fear: for thy judgments are good.

40 Behold, I have longed after thy precepts: quicken me in thy righteousness.

Hey means "window" in Hebrew. Windows admit light. To shine light into one's heart and thinking, we achieve comprehension. With that comprehension, we are capable of influencing our lives for the better. Hey, therefore, is about mastery and being the best at what we choose to be. Hey rules the right arm and is the color metallic violet.

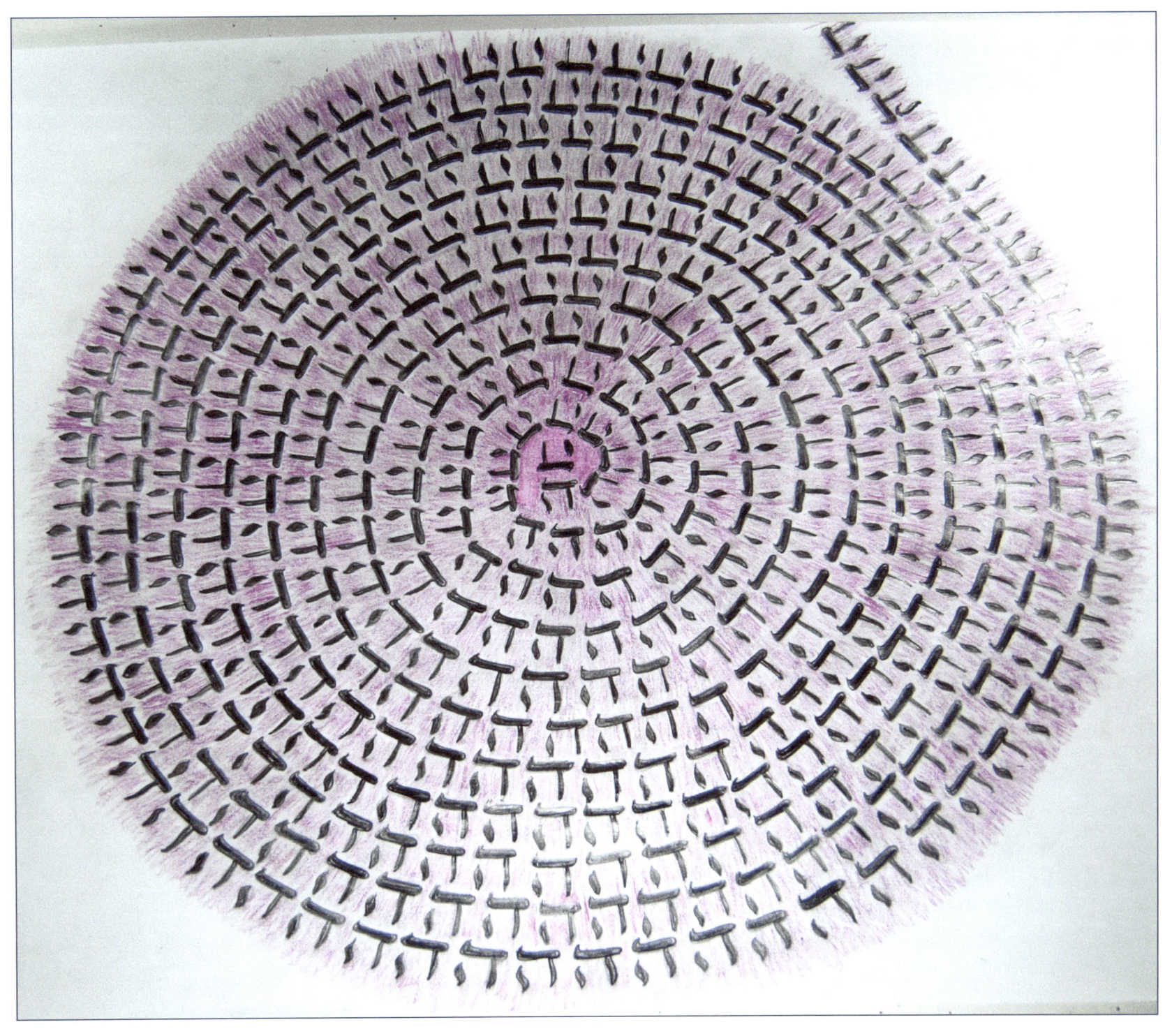

Vav asks God to be considered as the letter to initiate the creation of the world, stating she is one of the letters of that make up His Name. God, addressing Vav—but including Hey, another letter in His Name, in his answer—says that, for this reason, it is not possible for either of them to be considered, and that they should be satisfied that they both are part of His Name.

Psalm 119, verses, 41-48
VAV

41 Let thy mercies come also unto me, O LORD, even thy salvation, according to thy word.

42 So shall I have wherewith to answer him that reproacheth me: for I trust in thy word.

43 And take not the word of truth utterly out of my mouth; for I have hoped in thy judgments.

44 So shall I keep thy law continually for ever and ever.

45 And I will walk at liberty: for I seek thy precepts.

46 I will speak of thy testimonies also before kings, and will not be ashamed.

47 And I will delight myself in thy commandments, which I have loved.

48 My hands also will I lift up unto thy commandments, which I have loved; and I will meditate in thy statutes.

Vav means "nail" in Hebrew; it is therefore about uniting two separate objects—Vav as the letter "u" allows us to slowly correct our behavior; Vav as "w" (there is no letter "v" in Hebrew) is about working on the level of consciousness. The two concepts united allow one to achieve a higher intuition. As "u", Vav is the letter that rules the pancreas and is the color black. As "w", Vav rules the colon and rectum, and is the color lilac.

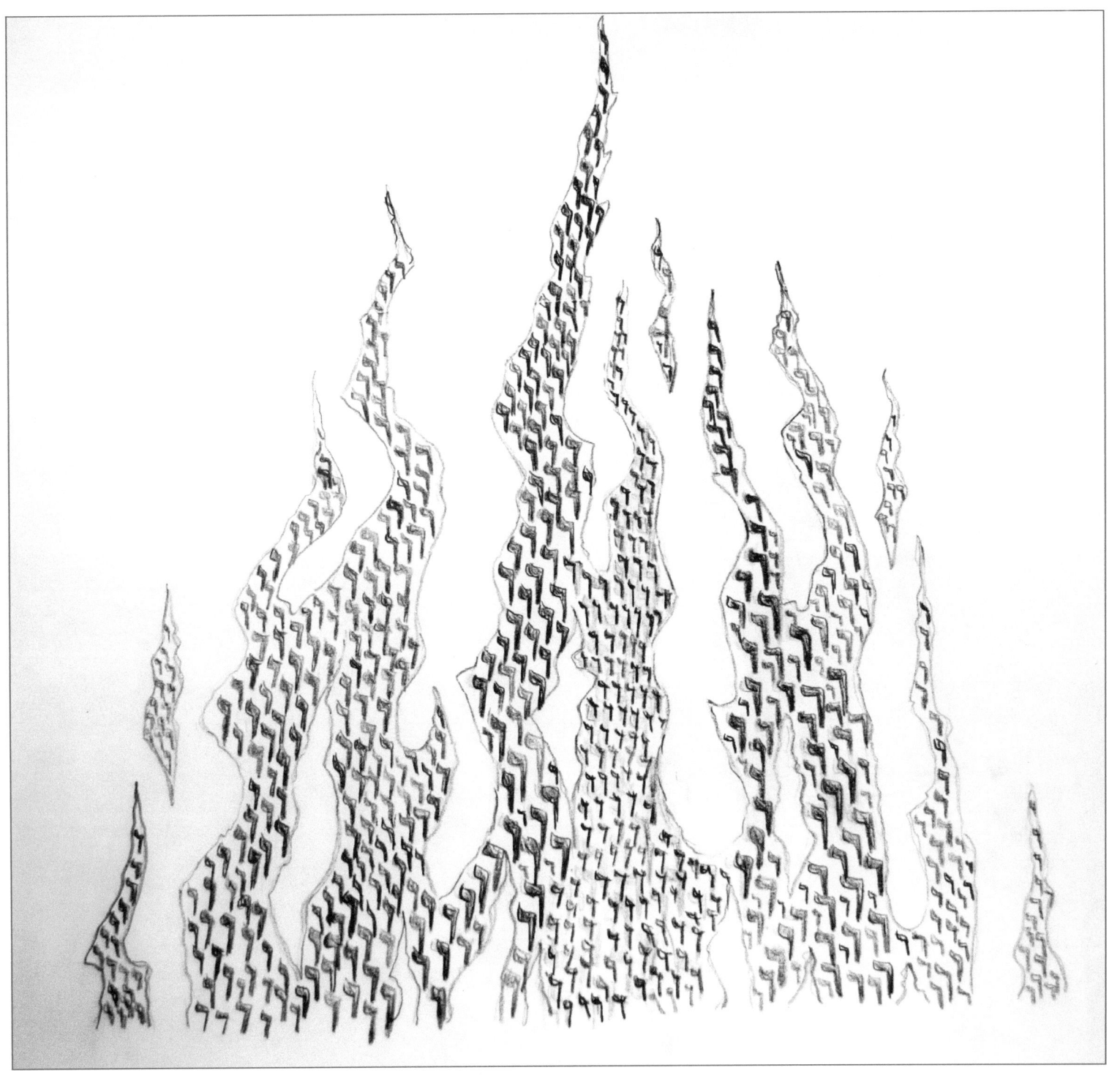

ZAYIN ASKS GOD to consider using her to create the world because she represents the observance of the Sabbath, *zachor*. God answers no, because Zayin also means "sword" and therefore represents war and is not appropriate for beginning the world.

Psalm 119, verses 49–56

ZAYIN

49 Remember the word unto thy servant, upon which thou hast caused me to hope.

50 This is my comfort in my affliction: for thy word hath quickened me.

51 The proud have had me greatly in derision: yet have I not declined from thy law.

52 I remembered thy judgments of old, O LORD; and have comforted myself.

53 Horror hath taken hold upon me because of the wicked that forsake thy law.

54 Thy statutes have been my songs in the house of my pilgrimage.

55 I have remembered thy name, O LORD, in the night, and have kept thy law.

56 This I had, because I kept thy precepts.

Because Zayin means "sword" in Hebrew, it is sharp enough to harm, but also useful in cutting through confusion and bringing clarity to a situation, a way of disentangling oneself from bad habits that get in the way of thriving. It has the quality of healing the heart, and its color is lemon yellow.

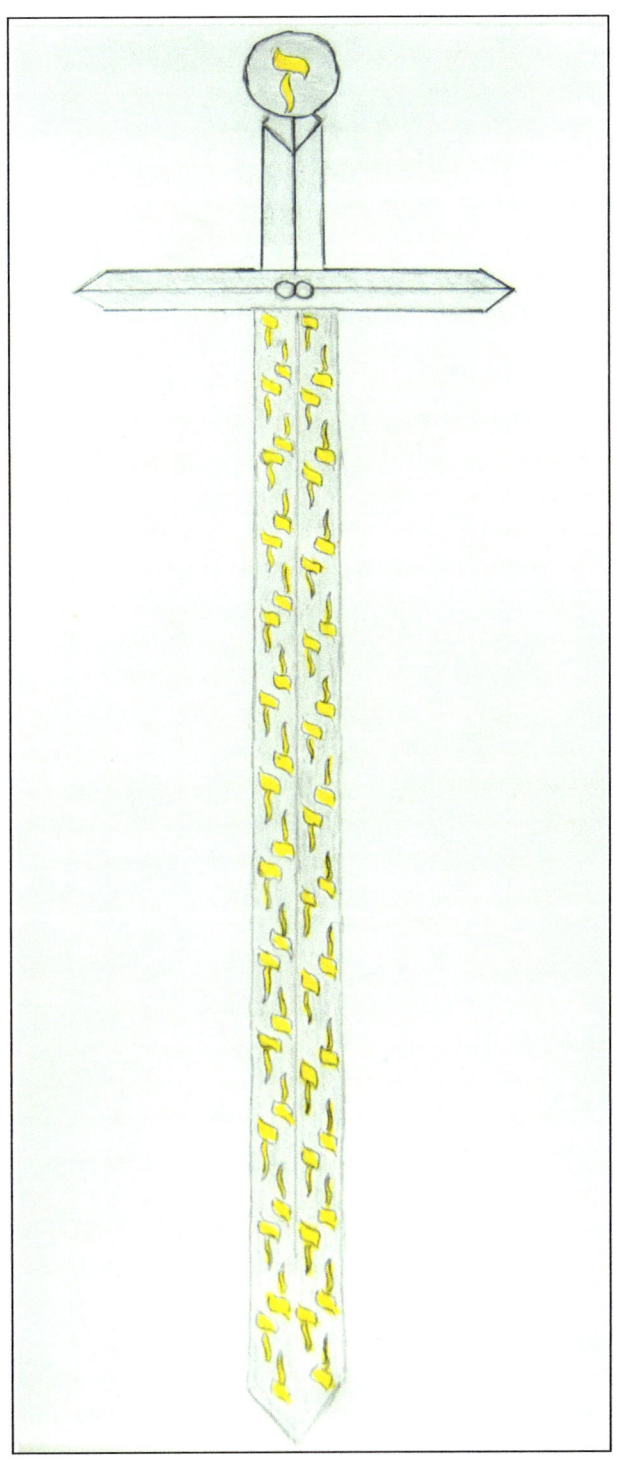

CHET IS INCLUDED in God's denial of Teth's request to be used to create the world. God says that both letters are part of the Hebrew word for "sin" and therefore cannot be candidates for initiating the creation of the world. And because they spell "sin", these two letters do not appear in the names of the twelve tribes of Israel.

Psalm 119, verses 57–64

CHET

57 Thou art my portion, O LORD: I have said that I would keep thy words.

58 I intreated thy favour with my whole heart: be merciful unto me according to thy word.

59 I thought on my ways, and turned my feet unto thy testimonies.

60 I made haste, and delayed not to keep thy commandments.

61 The bands of the wicked have robbed me: but I have not forgotten thy law.

62 At midnight I will rise to give thanks unto thee because of thy righteous judgments.

63 I am a companion of all them that fear thee, and of them that keep thy precepts.

64 The earth, O LORD, is full of thy mercy: teach me thy statutes.

Chet means "field" in Hebrew. This letter expresses the quality of infusing us with love, selflessness, and fearlessness. All three elements, along with the desire to unite with the Divine, are the foundation of enlightenment, the place where a joyous life can be planted and nurtured into being. Chet rules the stomach and is the color bloody red.

GOD ALSO DENIES Teth's request to be chosen to create the world. In addition to Teth and Chet spelling the word "sin" in Hebrew, God says no to Teth even though Teth is the initial letter in the word *tov*, Hebrew for "good". God explains that Teth's goodness is hidden and cannot take part in the world He is about to create.

Psalm 119, verses 65–72

TETH

65 Thou hast dealt well with thy servant, O LORD, according unto thy word.

66 Teach me good judgment and knowledge: for I have believed thy commandments.

67 Before I was afflicted I went astray: but now have I kept thy word.

68 Thou art good, and doest good; teach me thy statutes.

69 The proud have forged a lie against me: but I will keep thy precepts with my whole heart.

70 Their heart is as fat as grease; but I delight in thy law.

71 It is good for me that I have been afflicted; that I might learn thy statutes.

72 The law of thy mouth is better unto me than thousands of gold and silver.

Teth means "snake" in Hebrew. The snake is a symbol of both evil and wisdom across many cultures. It is through our mistakes that we have the opportunity to achieve redemption. Experiences—good, bad, and indifferent—in the end make us wiser. With this wisdom, we learn to be able to say what we mean and mean what we say, thus achieving understanding on a deeper level. It is the color of brown-black.

YUD APPROACHES GOD to be considered as the letter to initiate the creation of the world, pointing out that she is the first letter of His Name, Yehovah. God replies no; precisely because she is the beginning of His name, she cannot be spared for any other task.

Psalm 119, verses 73–80

YUD

73 Thy hands have made me and fashioned me: give me understanding, that I may learn thy commandments.

74 They that fear thee will be glad when they see me; because I have hoped in thy word.

75 I know, O LORD, that thy judgments are right, and that thou in faithfulness hast afflicted me.

76 Let, I pray thee, thy merciful kindness be for my comfort, according to thy word unto thy servant.

77 Let thy tender mercies come unto me, that I may live: for thy law is my delight.

78 Let the proud be ashamed; for they dealt perversely with me without a cause: but I will meditate in thy precepts.

79 Let those that fear thee turn unto me, and those that have known thy testimonies.

80 Let my heart be sound in thy statutes; that I be not ashamed.

Yud means "hand" in Hebrew. With your hands you can fashion what you desire, altering your physical, emotional, or mental behavior so you can develop the skill to self-heal. Yod as "i" heals the left kidney, as "j" the diaphragm, and as "y" the emotional aspects of the heart. The colors are light opal, dark opal, and light pink, respectively.

Kaph asks God to initiate the creation of the world through her because she is part of the Hebrew word for "honor", *kabod*. But God says no, because Kaph is also begins the word *kelayah*, "extermination", and would therefore not be an appropriate choice to initiate the creation of the world.

Psalm 119, verses 81–88

KAPH

81 My soul fainteth for thy salvation: but I hope in thy word.

82 Mine eyes fail for thy word, saying, When wilt thou comfort me?

83 For I am become like a bottle in the smoke; yet do I not forget thy statutes.

84 How many are the days of thy servant? when wilt thou execute judgment on them that persecute me?

85 The proud have digged pits for me, which are not after thy law.

86 All thy commandments are faithful: they persecute me wrongfully; help thou me.

87 They had almost consumed me upon earth; but I forsook not thy precepts.

88 Quicken me after thy lovingkindness; so shall I keep the testimony of thy mouth.

Kaph means "hand grasping" in Hebrew. It expresses the quality of manifestation, and of healing through effort and humility. This kind of healing takes time because it includes acknowledging one's mistakes and making an effort to overcome and correct them. It rules the left ear and is the color metallic blue.

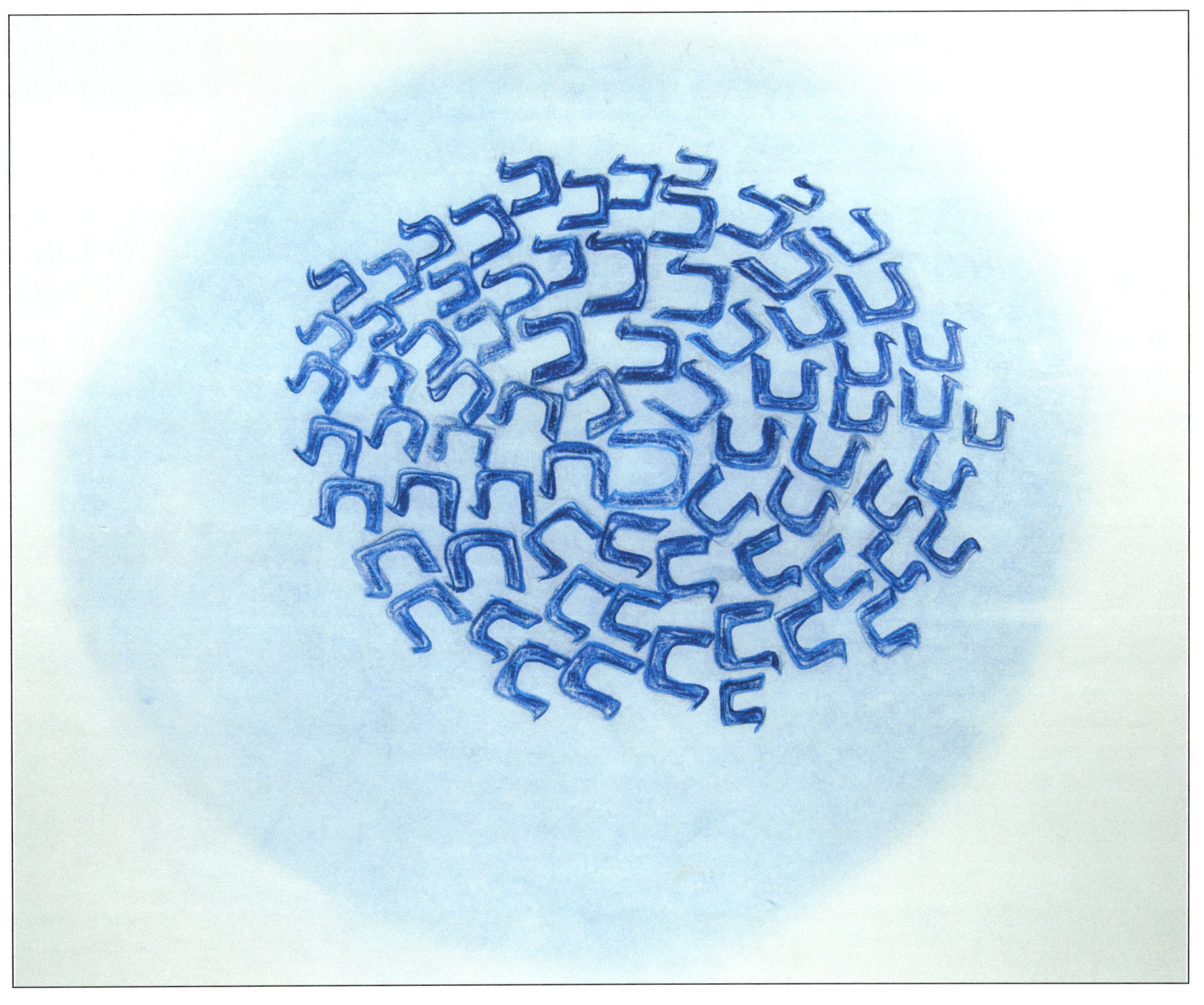

GOD WILL NOT CONSIDER Lamed, Mem, or Kaph for initiating the creation of the world because the three letters are needed to spell the word "king", *melekh*, and cannot be otherwise spared, since the world needs rulers.

Psalm 119, verses 89–96

LAMED

89 For ever, O LORD, thy word is settled in heaven.

90 Thy faithfulness is unto all generations: thou hast established the earth, and it abideth.

91 They continue this day according to thine ordinances: for all are thy servants.

92 Unless thy law had been my delights, I should then have perished in mine affliction.

93 I will never forget thy precepts: for with them thou hast quickened me.

94 I am thine, save me; for I have sought thy precepts.

95 The wicked have waited for me to destroy me: but I will consider thy testimonies.

96 I have seen an end of all perfection: but thy commandment is exceeding broad.

Lamed means "ox-goad" in Hebrew. Lamed is the letter of beauty, enabling us to see it everywhere we choose. This divine realization that beauty surrounds us, no matter what is happening, prods us forward to seek out a better life. Lamed rules the spleen and is the color dark green.

MEM APPROACHES GOD to be considered as the letter to initiate creating the world, since she begins word *melekh*, "king", and therefore would be an appropriate choice. God says no because the world needs a king.

Psalm 119, verses 97-104

MEM

97 O how love I thy law! it is my meditation all the day.

98 Thou through thy commandments hast made me wiser than mine enemies: for they are ever with me.

99 I have more understanding than all my teachers: for thy testimonies are my meditation.

100 I understand more than the ancients, because I keep thy precepts.

101 I have refrained my feet from every evil way, that I might keep thy word.

102 I have not departed from thy judgments: for thou hast taught me.

103 How sweet are thy words unto my taste! yea, sweeter than honey to my mouth!

104 Through thy precepts I get understanding: therefore I hate every false way.

Mem means "seas" or "water" in Hebrew. The element water is linked to emotions, and Mem is a healer of all emotions. If you can harness your emotions and think clearly, you can direct your energy to nurture your creativity instead. Mem rules the space of the abdomen without the organs, and is the color blue-green.

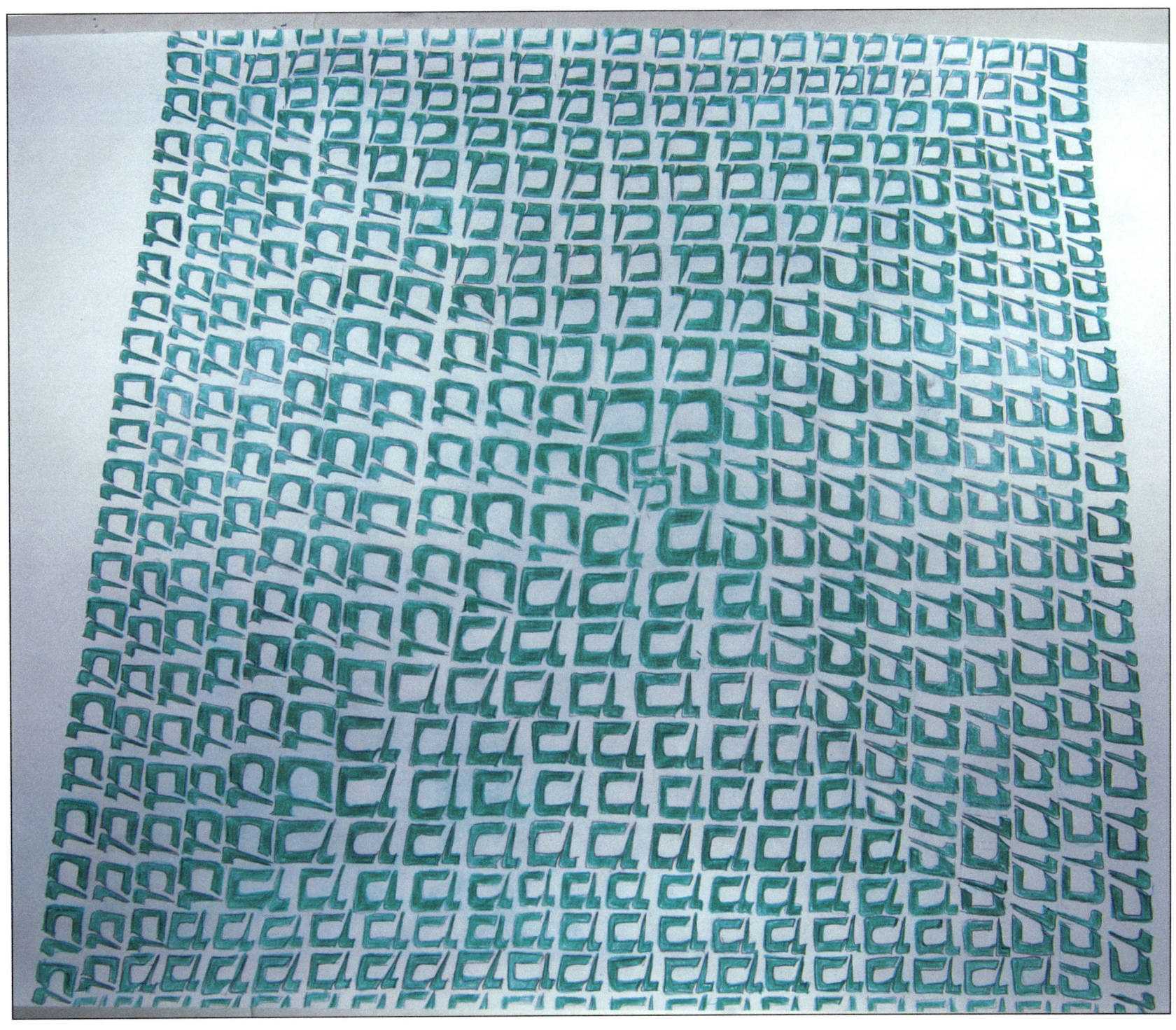

Nun asks to be considered for the honor of initiating the world because she begins the Hebrew words "fearful", *nora*, as well as "comely", *naga*. God answers no because she also begins the word "fall", *nofelim*, which is not an appropriate energy for creating the world.

Psalm 119, verses 105-112

NUN

105 Thy word is a lamp unto my feet, and a light unto my path.

106 I have sworn, and I will perform it, that I will keep thy righteous judgments.

107 I am afflicted very much: quicken me, O LORD, according unto thy word.

108 Accept, I beseech thee, the freewill offerings of my mouth, O LORD, and teach me thy judgments.

109 My soul is continually in my hand: yet do I not forget thy law.

110 The wicked have laid a snare for me: yet I erred not from thy precepts.

111 Thy testimonies have I taken as an heritage for ever: for they are the rejoicing of my heart.

112 I have inclined mine heart to perform thy statutes always, even unto the end.

Nun means "fish" in Hebrew. Fish are a symbol of fertility and abundance. The letter nun represents the quality of bliss. Fertility, abundance, and bliss all carry a person forward in achieving enlightenment. Nun heals the liver and is the color red.

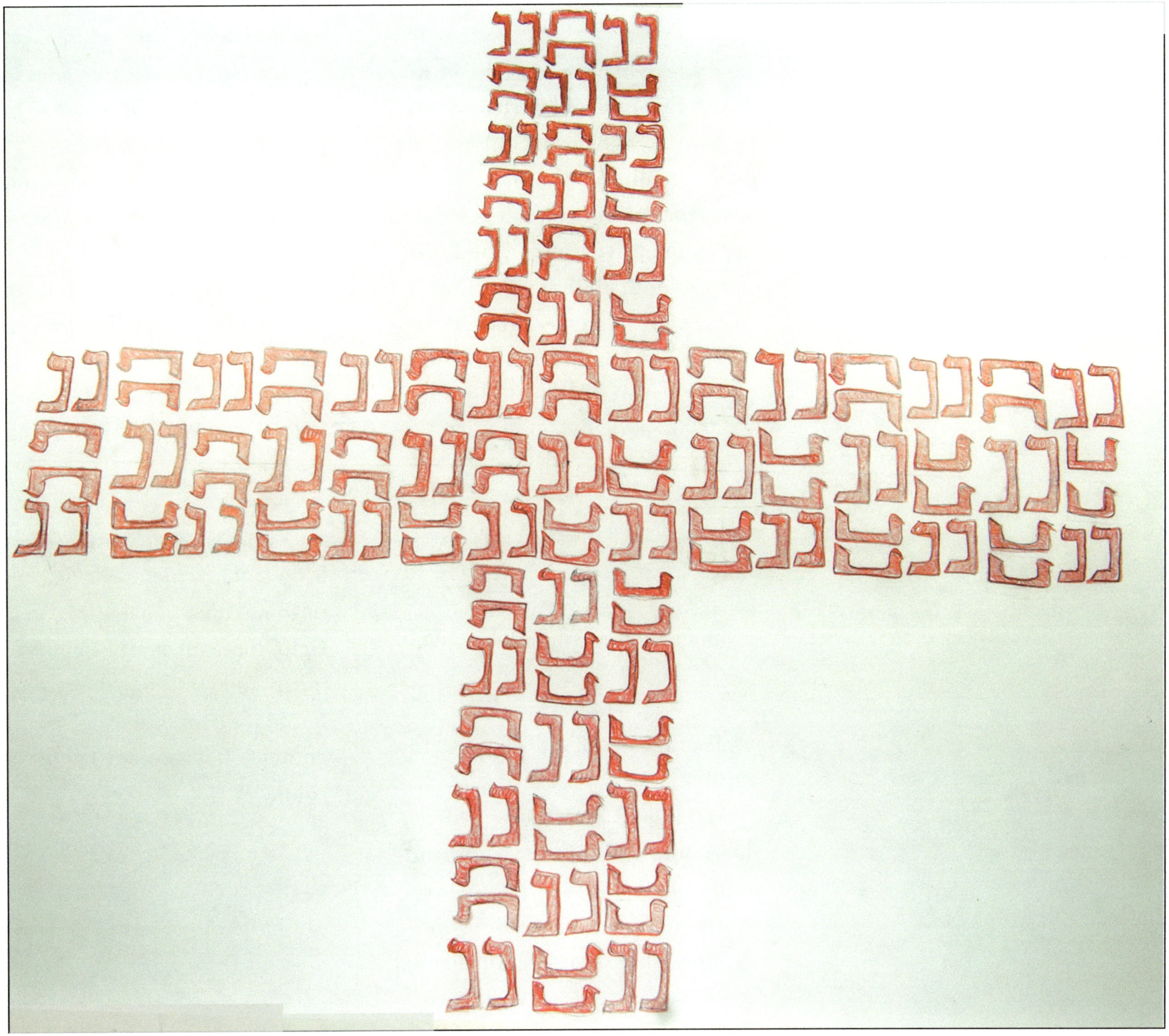

SAMECH APPROACHES GOD to be considered as the letter through which He creates the world. She points out her purpose is to uphold the "fallen", *samekah* in Hebrew, as it is written in Psalm 145, verse 14: "The Lord upholdeth all that fall." God replies that, for this very reason, Samech must remain available for those who need to be upheld.

Psalm 119, verses 113–120

SAMECH

113 I hate vain thoughts: but thy law do I love.

114 Thou art my hiding place and my shield: I hope in thy word.

115 Depart from me, ye evildoers: for I will keep the commandments of my God.

116 Uphold me according unto thy word, that I may live: and let me not be ashamed of my hope.

117 Hold thou me up, and I shall be safe: and I will have respect unto thy statutes continually.

118 Thou hast trodden down all them that err from thy statutes: for their deceit is falsehood.

119 Thou puttest away all the wicked of the earth like dross: therefore I love thy testimonies.

120 My flesh trembleth for fear of thee; and I am afraid of thy judgments.

Samech means "tent peg" in Hebrew—that which secures a tent to its foundation and helps keep it upright. Samech has the quality of humility and gratitude, the required foundation for one seeking enlightenment. It is a muted bright red in color.

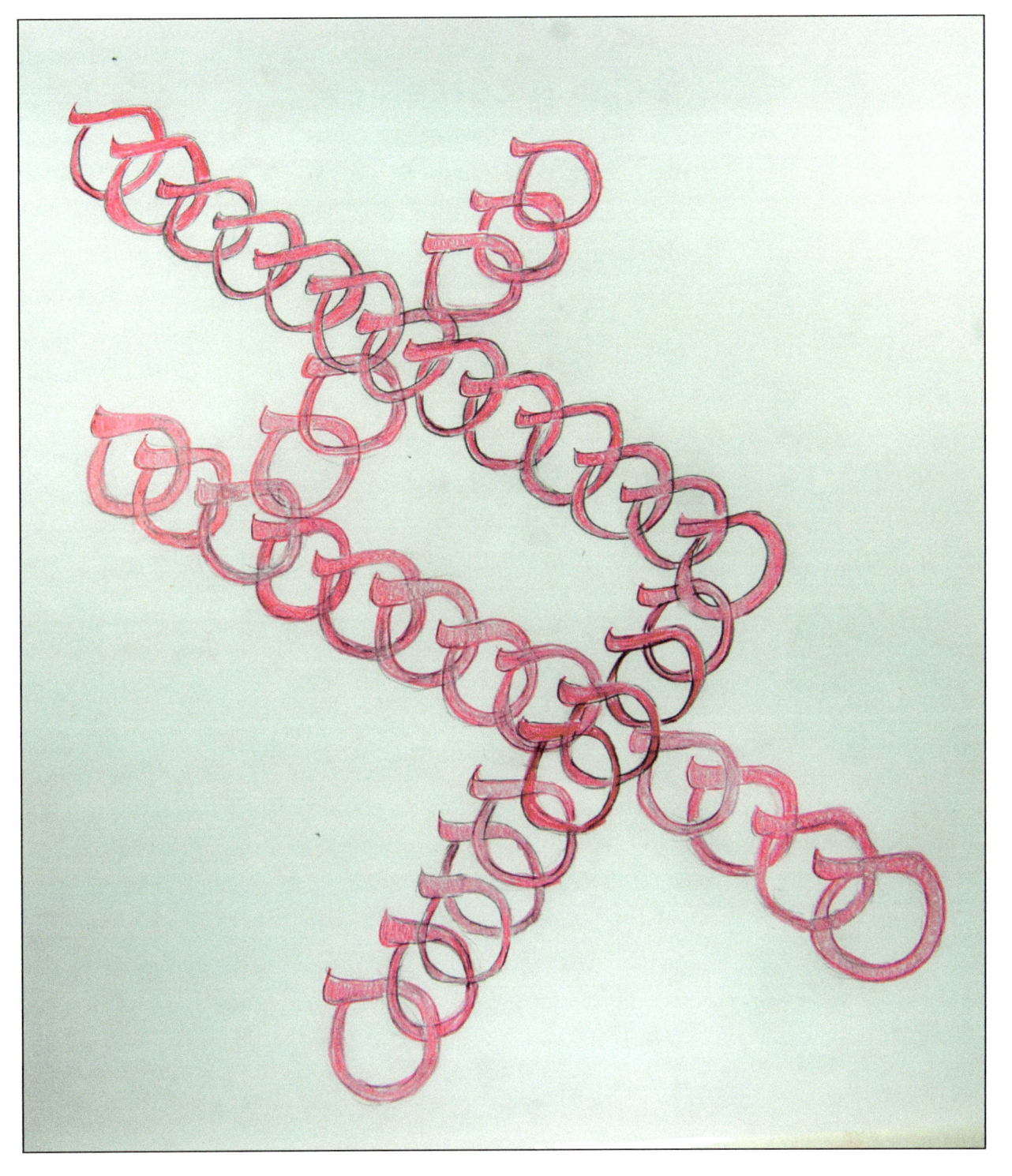

GOD REFUSES AYIN her request to be used to create the world. While she begins the Hebrew word *anavah*, which means "humility", she also begins the Hebrew word *awon*, "iniquity".

Psalm 119, verse 121-128

AYIN

121 I have done judgment and justice: leave me not to mine oppressors.

122 Be surety for thy servant for good: let not the proud oppress me.

123 Mine eyes fail for thy salvation, and for the word of thy righteousness.

124 Deal with thy servant according unto thy mercy, and teach me thy statutes.

125 I am thy servant; give me understanding, that I may know thy testimonies.

126 It is time for thee, LORD, to work: for they have made void thy law.

127 Therefore I love thy commandments above gold; yea, above fine gold.

128 Therefore I esteem all thy precepts concerning all things to be right; and I hate every false way.

Ayin means "eye" in Hebrew. It has the quality of creating justice and balance. Justice, when tempered by judgment—that is, the ability to refrain from judging others unless you have walked in their shoes—allows us to gain the balance needed to achieve a far-reaching vision of true justice: compassion. Ayin heals the throat and is the color ultramarine blue.

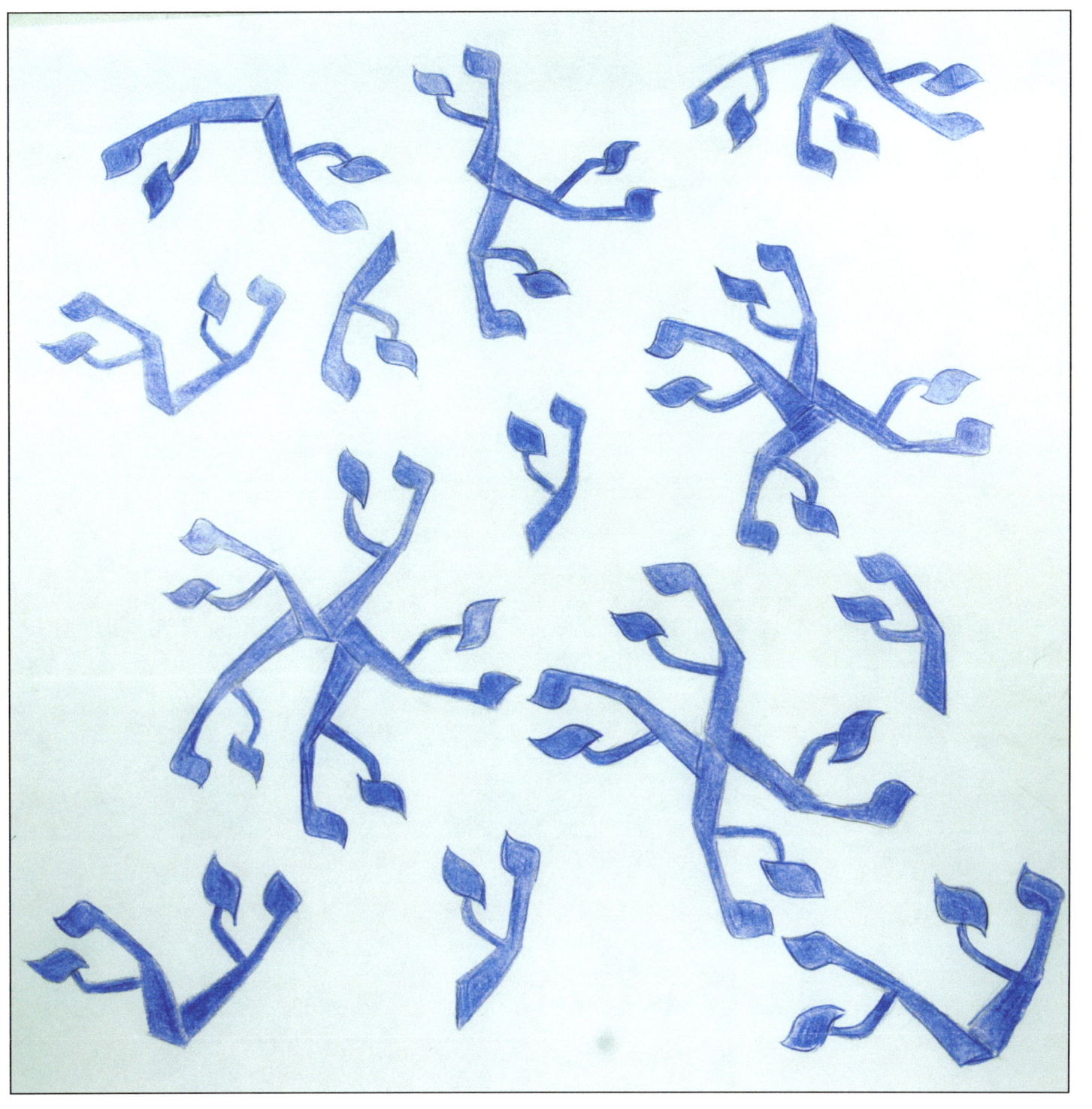

Pey approaches God to be considered as the letter He uses to create the world because she begins the Hebrew words *purkana* and *peduth*, which mean "redemption" and "deliverance." God concedes these are good reasons to be chosen, but since Pey also begins the word *pesha*, "transgression", He tells her no.

Psalm 119, verse 129–136

PEY

129 Thy testimonies are wonderful: therefore doth my soul keep them.

130 The entrance of thy words giveth light; it giveth understanding unto the simple.

131 I opened my mouth, and panted: for I longed for thy commandments.

132 Look thou upon me, and be merciful unto me, as thou usest to do unto those that love thy name.

133 Order my steps in thy word: and let not any iniquity have dominion over me.

134 Deliver me from the oppression of man: so will I keep thy precepts.

135 Make thy face to shine upon thy servant; and teach me thy statutes.

136 Rivers of waters run down mine eyes, because they keep not thy law.

Pey means "mouth" in Hebrew. This letter has the quality of humility as spiritual perfection. It rules the right nostril and is the color of dark gray.

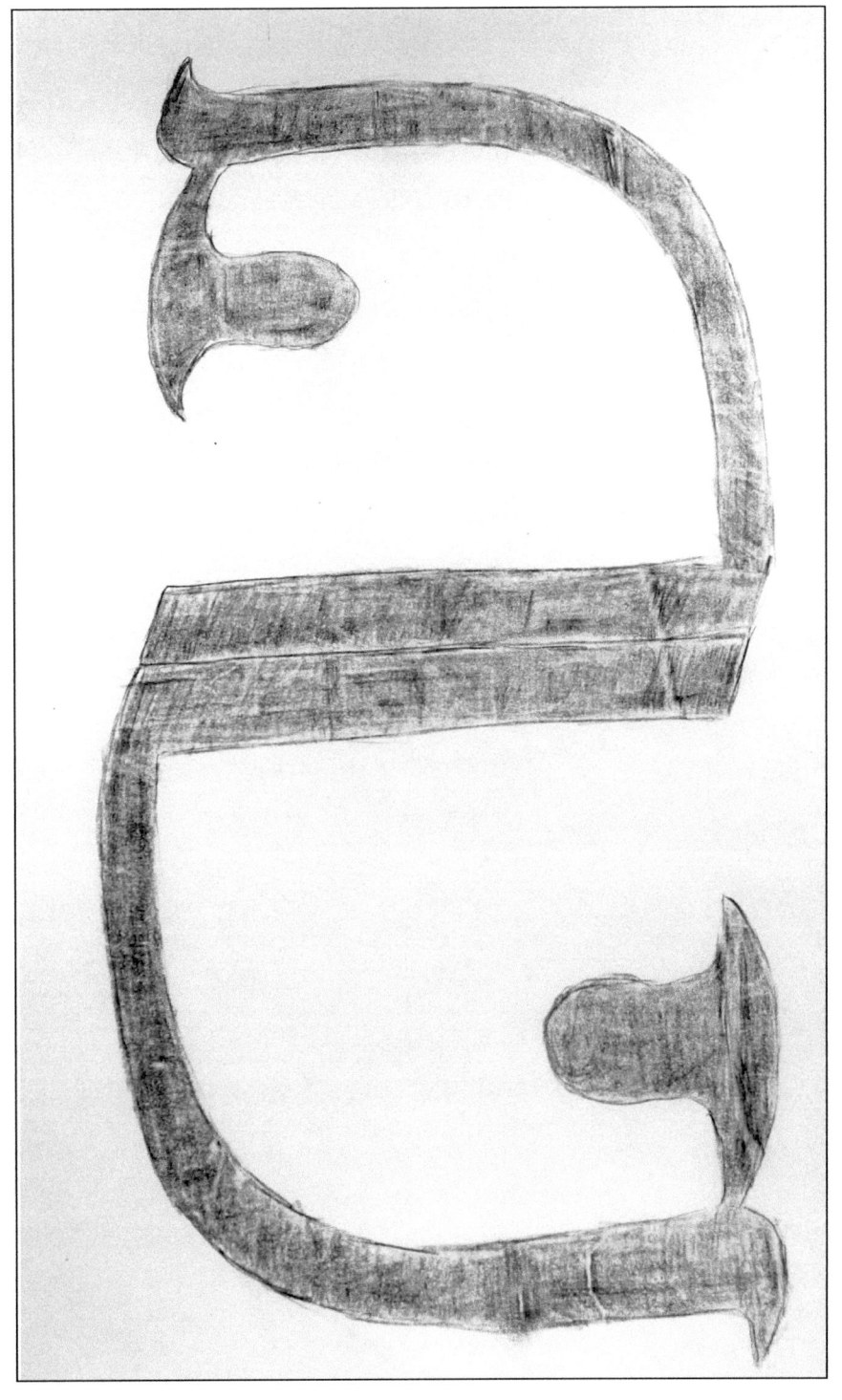

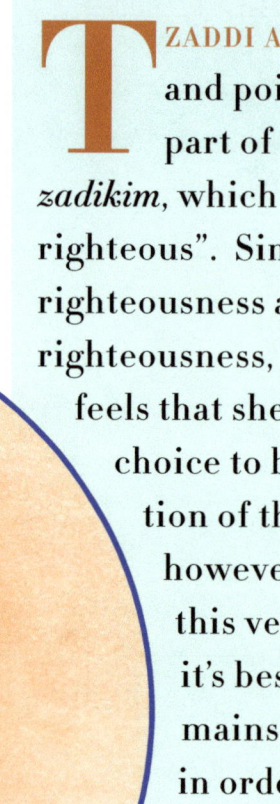

TZADDI APPROACHES GOD and points out she is part of the Hebrew word *zadikim*, which means "the righteous". Since the Lord is righteousness and also loves righteousness, she therefore feels that she would be a good choice to begin the creation of the world. God, however, answers that this very quality means it's best that she remains mostly hidden, in order not to give offense to humanity.

Psalm 119, verses 137–144
TZADDI

137 Righteous art thou, O LORD, and upright are thy judgments.

138 Thy testimonies that thou hast commanded are righteous and very faithful.

139 My zeal hath consumed me, because mine enemies have forgotten thy words.

140 Thy word is very pure: therefore thy servant loveth it.

141 I am small and despised: yet do not I forget thy precepts.

142 Thy righteousness is an everlasting righteousness, and thy law is the truth.

143 Trouble and anguish have taken hold on me: yet thy commandments are my delights.

144 The righteousness of thy testimonies is everlasting: give me understanding, and I shall live.

Tzaddi means "fish hook" in Hebrew. It reflects the ability to understand enlightenment by acquiring the humility to sift through one's subconscious, face oneself, and as a result be able to define one's personal truth. The color is reddish brown.

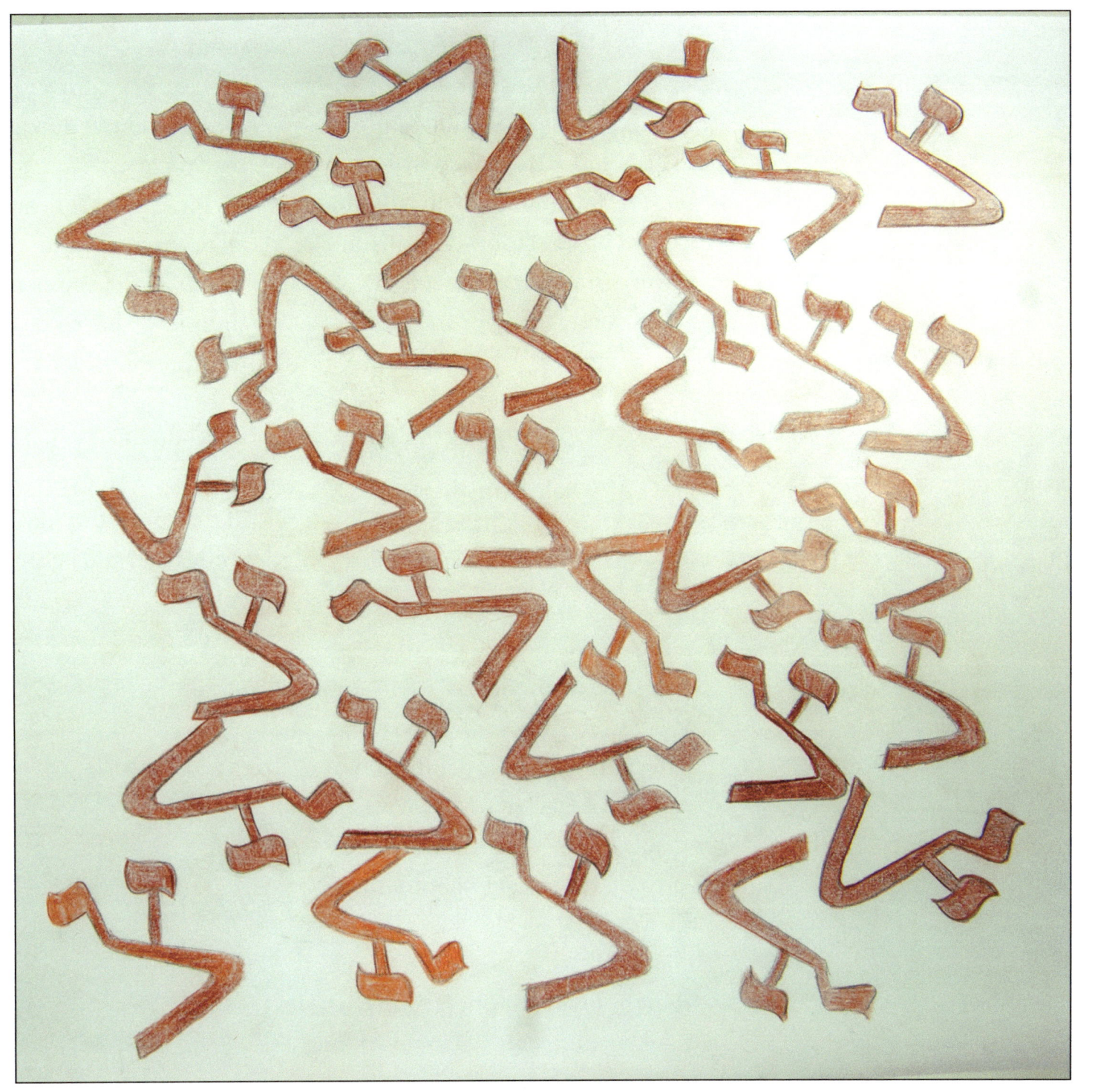

God denies Koph, along with Resh and Shin, all three of which combine to create the Hebrew word *sheker*, "falsehood", a quality that cannot be considered to initiate the creation of the world.

Psalm 119, verses 145–152
KOPH

145 I cried with my whole heart; hear me, O LORD: I will keep thy statutes.

146 I cried unto thee; save me, and I shall keep thy testimonies.

147 I prevented the dawning of the morning, and cried: I hoped in thy word.

148 Mine eyes prevent the night watches, that I might meditate in thy word.

149 Hear my voice according unto thy lovingkindness: O LORD, quicken me according to thy judgment.

150 They draw nigh that follow after mischief: they are far from thy law.

151 Thou art near, O LORD; and all thy commandments are truth.

152 Concerning thy testimonies, I have known of old that thou hast founded them for ever.

Koph means "back of the head" in Hebrew. It expresses the quality of realization, of making a wish come true, and is silver blue in color.

GOD WILL NOT TAKE RESH into consideration for launching the creation of the world for the same reason: the three letters—Resh, Koph, and Shin—allude to "falsehood". At best, they support each other to balance out the negativity of falsehood by also spelling the Hebrew word *kesher*, which means "strengthening".

Psalm 119, verses 153-160

RESH

153 Consider mine affliction, and deliver me: for I do not forget thy law.

154 Plead my cause, and deliver me: quicken me according to thy word.

155 Salvation is far from the wicked: for they seek not thy statutes.

156 Great are thy tender mercies, O LORD: quicken me according to thy judgments.

157 Many are my persecutors and mine enemies; yet do I not decline from thy testimonies.

158 I beheld the transgressors, and was grieved; because they kept not thy word.

159 Consider how I love thy precepts: quicken me, O LORD, according to thy lovingkindness.

160 Thy word is true from the beginning: and every one of thy righteous judgments endureth for ever.

Resh means "head" in Hebrew. It embodies authority, genius, the highest intellect, and understanding the most difficult concepts. Resh is therefore the key to reaching inspired knowledge. Resh rules the left nostril and is the color gold.

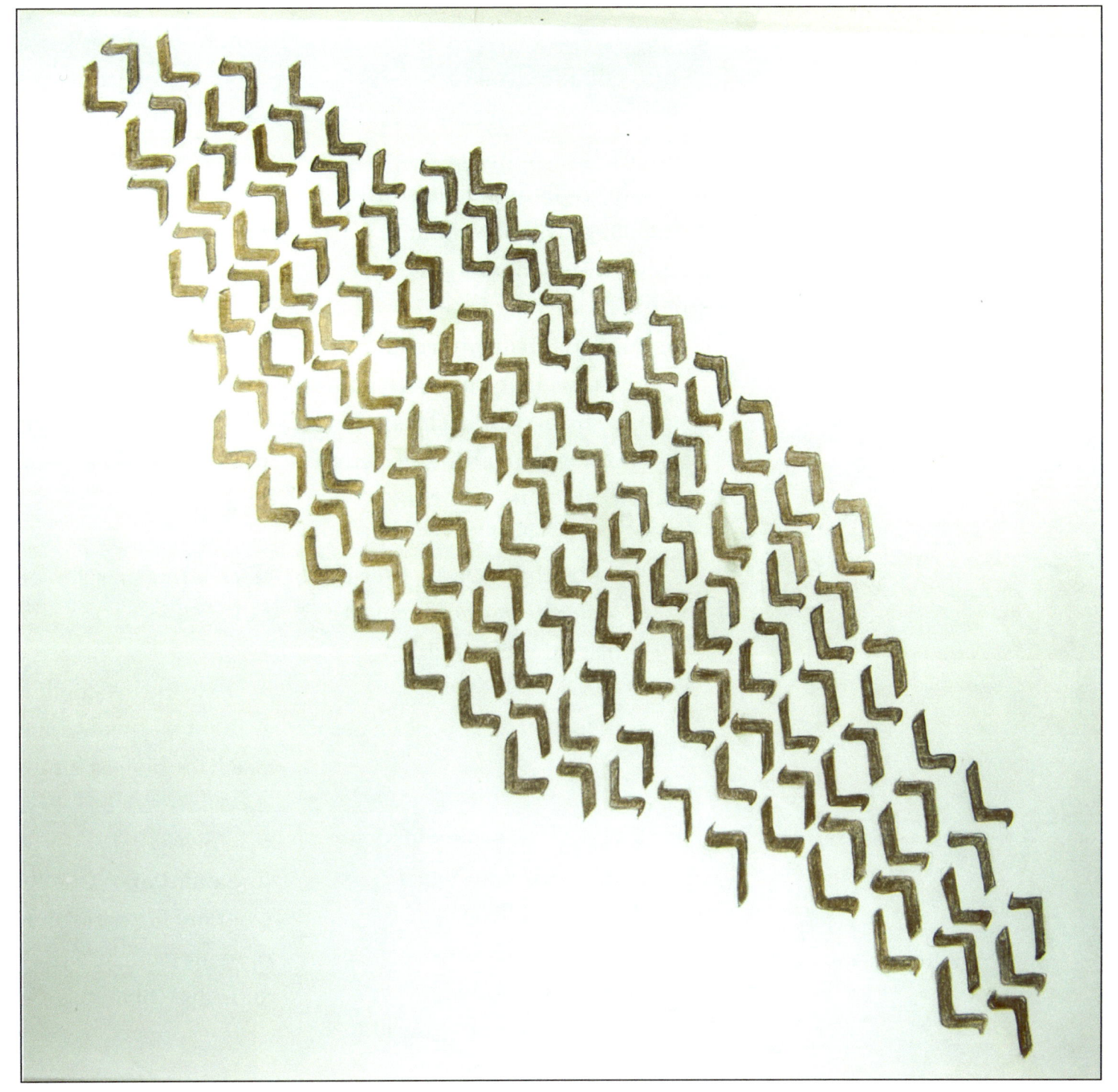

When Shin comes before God to be considered as the letter to initiate the creation of the world, she gives as her reason that she begins the God name Shaddai, which means "Almighty". God acknowledges this is good and true but rejects her as well because, with Resh and Koph, she spells *sheker*; and although Shin is the letter of truth, every good lie has a bit of truth in it, and, therefore, she cannot be used to create the world.

Psalm 119, verses 161-168
SHIN

161 Princes have persecuted me without a cause: but my heart standeth in awe of thy word.

162 I rejoice at thy word, as one that findeth great spoil.

163 I hate and abhor lying: but thy law do I love.

164 Seven times a day do I praise thee because of thy righteous judgments.

165 Great peace have they which love thy law: and nothing shall offend them.

166 LORD, I have hoped for thy salvation, and done thy commandments.

167 My soul hath kept thy testimonies; and I love them exceedingly.

168 I have kept thy precepts and thy testimonies: for all my ways are before thee.

Shin means "tooth" in Hebrew. It is about sharpening one's ability to reach the highest intuition, perhaps even the capacity for clairvoyance, all of which fuels a sense of discernment (the ability of separating out what is true) and furthers spiritual development. Shin heals the gallbladder and is the color burgundy red.

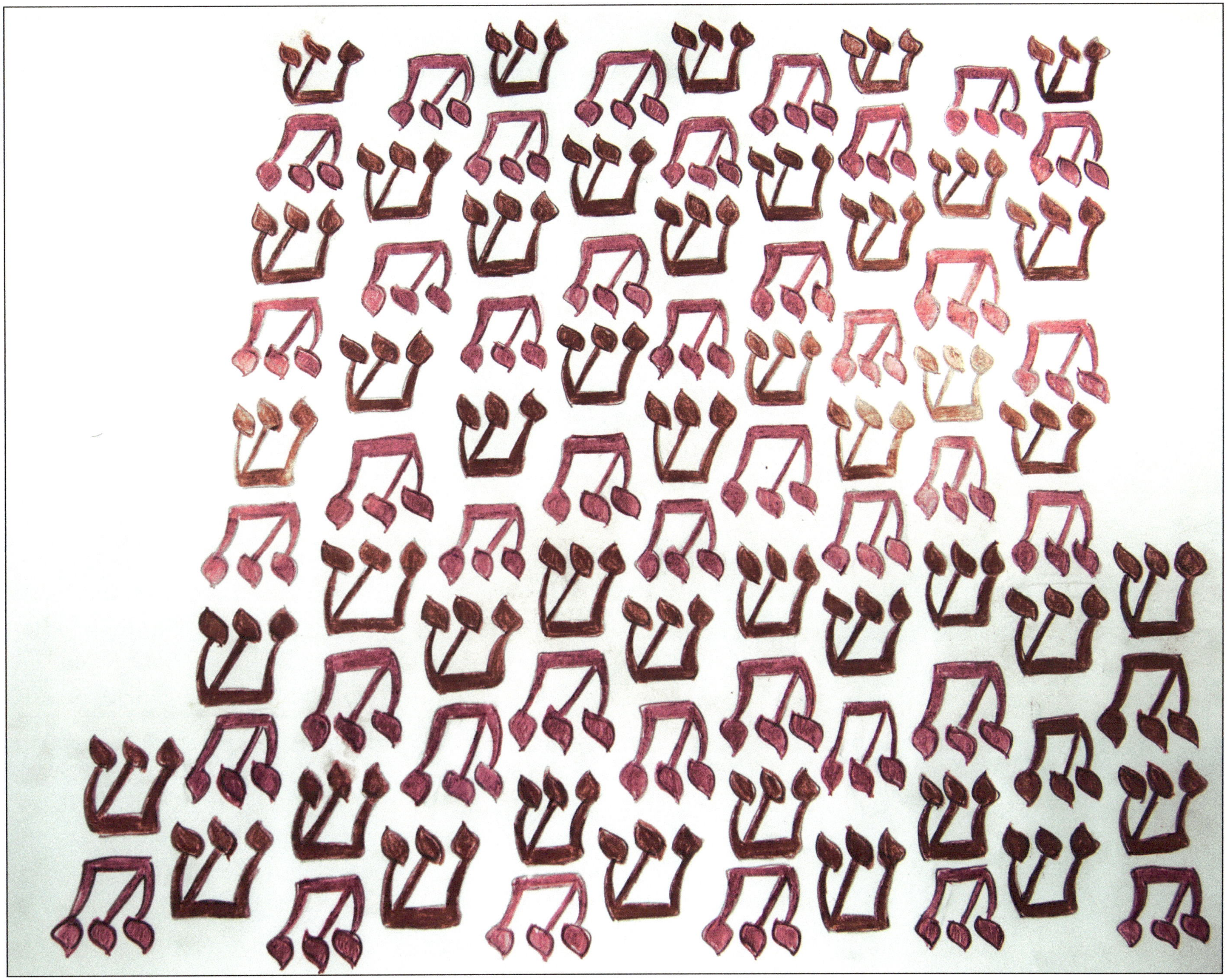

TAV APPROACHES GOD and asks to be chosen as the letter to initiate the creation of the world since she is the final letter of the Hebrew word *emet*, meaning "truth". God concedes this is an excellent reason to considered; however, Tav already has a special assignment, having been singled out as the letter to serve as a mark on the foreheads of those who have faithfully kept the law. In addition to this, Tav also is the final letter in *mavet*, Hebrew for "death"; therefore, God refuses Tav's request.

Psalm 119, verses 169–176
TAV

169 Let my cry come near before thee, O LORD: give me understanding according to thy word.

170 Let my supplication come before thee: deliver me according to thy word.

171 My lips shall utter praise, when thou hast taught me thy statutes.

172 My tongue shall speak of thy word: for all thy commandments are righteousness.

173 Let thine hand help me; for I have chosen thy precepts.

174 I have longed for thy salvation, O LORD; and thy law is my delight.

175 Let my soul live, and it shall praise thee; and let thy judgments help me.

176 I have gone astray like a lost sheep; seek thy servant; for I do not forget thy commandments.

Tav means "signature" or "mark" in Hebrew. It represents fertile enlightenment achieved through completion of efforts and perfection in understanding, which is now able to express itself in joyous fulfillment.

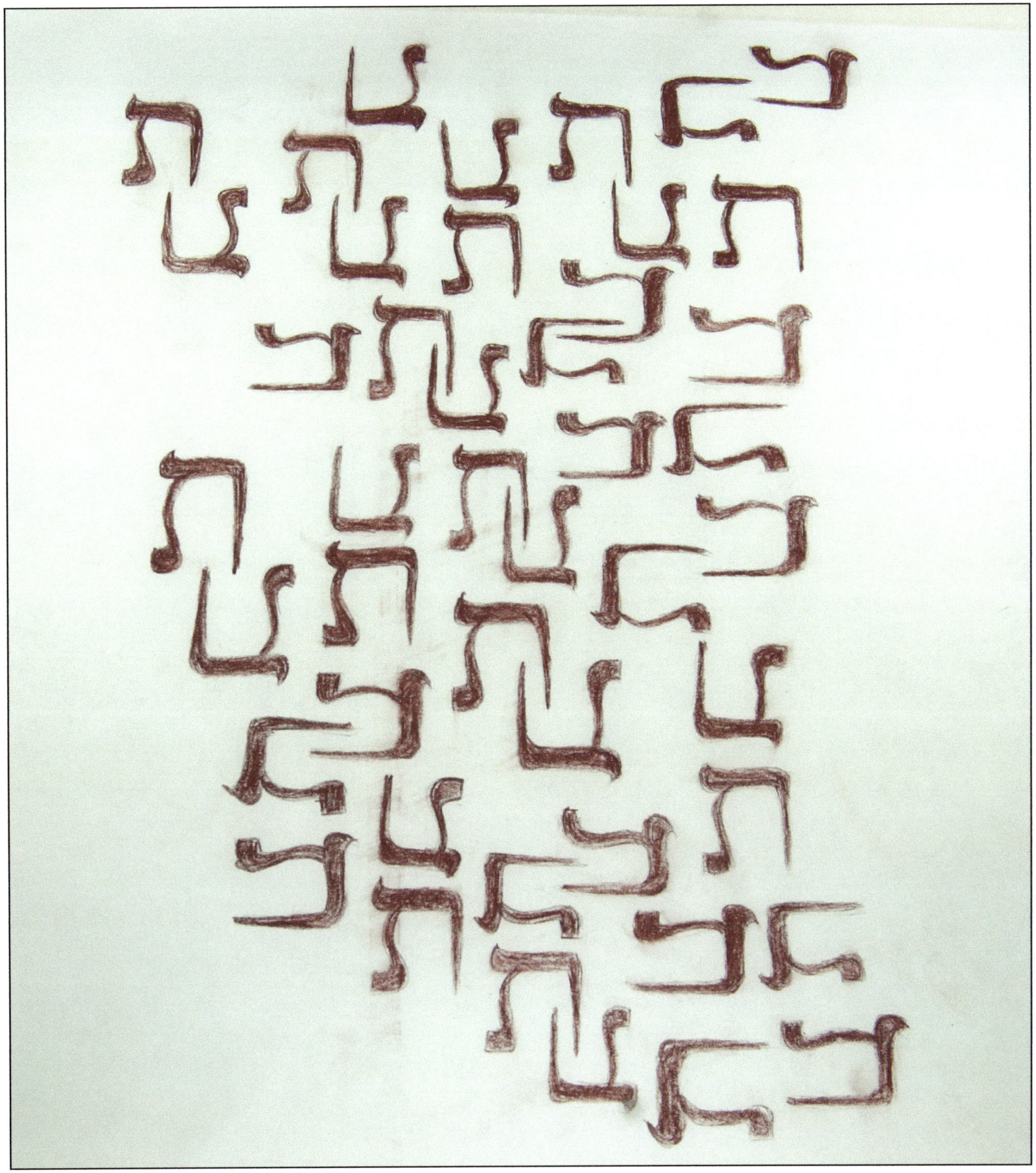

ABOUT THE AUTHOR

Eugenia Koukounas has degrees in both politics and nursing, has had a background in journalism, and writes both nonfiction and fiction. She has studied and practiced Taiji for fifteen years, Kaballah for sixteen, and Shamanism for twelve.

Ms. Koukounas has published widely in newspapers and magazines. Her first book-length work, *All Our Relations: One Path To Spiritual Devotion*, an Eric Hoffer Award Winner, appeared in 2017. She is currently at work on a modern tea-cozy entitled *Winslow's Promise*.

She lives with her husband, the novelist and poet Barry Sheinkopf, in Northern New Jersey.

www.ingramcontent.com/pod-product-compliance
Lightning Source LLC
Chambersburg PA
CBHW041951150426

43195CB00005B/107